S0-AAC-604

Call Me Myriad

Constance Hester

Copyright © 2004 by Constance Hester. All rights reserved. Printed in the United States of America. No part of this book may be used without written permission, except in the case of brief quotations embodied in critical articles and reviews. For information, contact the author at 1828 Dorothy N.E., Albuquerque, New Mexico 87112.

Book and cover design by Concepción Lopez-Cherry

Wildflower Press colophon designed by Sherri Holtke

Printed by Downtown Printing, Albuquerque, New Mexico

ISBN 0-9714343-8-7

The Wildflower Press

P. O. Box 4757
Albuquerque, New Mexico
87196-4757
www.thewildflowerpress.com

Acknowledgements

"A Purple Experience," "Golden Shroud," "Smothering," "Stringing Tobacco," and "Yellow School Bus Graveyard" were published in *Fresh Ink*.

"All the Sea Knows," "Oldest Book Shop in New Mexico," "Scabby Knees and Make-Up," "Silk Stockings — 1945," and "Starting With Rap" were included in *Fresh Ink II*.

"Race Ya" (as "A Particularly Seductive Stable Boy"), "Fool's Day," "Numinous," "Where Van Gogh Paints" (as "Put Your Ear Down to Your Soul and Listen Hard"), "Whatever They Say Must Be True," and "Women's Memories Are Long" were published in *Fresh Ink III*.

"Autumn Storm," "Chiles — Red Chiles," "Crumbling Adobe," "Jardín de los Tres Mujeres," "Song of Bones," "Taos Inn," and "Tell a Lie About Yourself" appeared in *Fresh Ink IV*.

"Behind the Window" (as "Cars Sleeping at the Curb"), "Ground Squirrels," and "I Missed It the First Time" were in *Fresh Ink V*.

"A Sky Falling Dream," "Dreaming of Snakes," and "The Meaning of Roses" were published in *Dream Machinery*.

"A Variety of Angels" appeared in *Orphic Lute*.

"Haiku" was in *Frog Pond*.

"Feminine Eyes" was published in *Poet Tree*.

"First Music Lesson" was in *Verve*.

"Call Me Myriad" (as "If Anyone From the Country Club…") appeared in *Tule Review*.

"In the Clutches of Roses" was published in *Mockingbird*.

"It's Me! Emma Goldberg" was included in *Across the Generations*.

"Mandala's Eye" and "When Butterflies Sing" were published in *Crazy Quilt*.

"Mother Tongue" was included in *Writing For Our Lives*.

"Native Dancers" appeared in *Milvia Street*.

"Puzzle Pieces" and "Shadow — A Ghazal" were in *Convolvulous*.

"The Diviner" was in *Central Avenue*.

"Triangle" was published in *Sacred River*.

Dedication

for my sons and their families

M. S. Stewart, Deja Stewart, Sabrina Stewart,
Erik Carlson, and Debbie Gilbert

Thanks...

My thanks to the writing teachers who taught me to write
with a "wild mind"; Natalie Goldberg, Joan Logghe, Cecelia
Moochnek, and Jannie Dresser. Also, my thanks to friends
and fellow writers who helped me by critiquing and editing
my work, including: Fresh Ink Poetry group, Mary Berg,
Adam David Miller, and Elise Peeples.

Contents

III. Rain

IV. Shadow

V. Light

VI. Picture

VII. Money

VIII. Ambition

Call Me Myriad

"If anyone from the country club
        asks you if you write poems..." *
...say your name is Short Shanks,
you don't know a poem
from a paean, have never held
a pen, never let ink spill
out of your arteries.

Tell the truth
about the hard sidewalk of life
and no one will believe you.
Say you remember them from
a past life in which you both

were whores in Mesopotamia,
wore gauze veils and nothing else,
shaved your pubic hair,
let the hair on your legs grow
long enough to braid. Tell them

your name is Sue and you are truly
blue — bluely true — to any man
for five minutes or never,
that you once sailed with Cortez
and the ship was lifted

into the air by a B52, set down
in Samoa, that you and Cortez
are the parents of all Samoans
and that he ate too much garlic.
Say you had one hundred children

by fifty husbands, your name is
Fruitful. Remember, they will never
know who you are, so the lies are more
truth than they need to hear. Remind
them you taught Chopin to play

the piano. When he played the scales,
got the fingering wrong, you bit him,
and he hated F#, refused to touch it.
Tell them he buried you, sang a tune
at your graveside. Say that nothing

is grave but everything is serious.
Tell them you're a looney tune
who only makes love to the man
in the moon who isn't a man at all
but a warrior woman with a pack of wolves

at her heels. Tell them you're a backache
and your name is Strain, that you're
a computer programmer who weaves carpets
on ancient looms, every carpet has a magic
spell that makes it fly. You must meditate

for three days to discover it,
then the spell will come to you.
You can fly into anyone's soul on your magic
carpet and be that person for a day.
You will become mad then, eat from garbage

cans — but it will taste like milk, honey
and strawberries. When the heater hums
in the crowded room and the carpet settles
onto polished floor, tell them
the name to which you answer

is Myriad.

* Tess Gallagher

I. Tongue

Tongue — A Ghazal*

I hold a deep yellow lemon in my palm, smell its fragrance.
I touch its fresh tang with tip of pink tongue.

A silver-backed gorilla, trailed by its clan, follows a path
through dense shrubs.
He pulls a leafy branch to his mouth, strips the leaves
with his tongue.

Locales of ancient grief and glory have long been the foci
of tourist pilgrimage.
The tourists should stand silent, not click-clack their
serpent tongues.

My granddaughter is being teased mercilessly
by schoolmates.
Cruelly, I long to take sharp scissors and snip their
twisted tongues.

Constance, you know of moving stories that you long to tell.
Remember, there are matters about which it is best to hold
your tongue.

The early Christian church and some later mystics claimed to
have a certain gift. They claimed the power of conversing in,
and understanding, unknown tongues.

Having fallen into enchantment, two lovers hold each other
with eyes.
Only later do they share the intimacy of tongues.

* A poetry form from India/Persia, composed of from five to seven
  couplets that end with the same word. Each couplet is a separate
  thought and in one of them the writer's name is mentioned.

Mother Tongue

The tongue of the mother taught you,
her tongue taught you to speak,
you speak in the tongue, with the tongue
of your mother, the mother who gave you
life, gave you speech, the private speech,
family speech, the speaking tongue
of the family that marks your place, makes
your place, connects you to your tribe,
your mothers, their tongues, their stories,
the stories of their lives, their tongues
telling, repeating, speaking the tongues
of the mothers through time, past time,
out of time, passed you their tongues,
their lives, their speech, your place.

Starting With Rap

Which ancestor gave us sound —
Made it possible for a mother
        to croon to her baby,
A father to call a warning
        to his too adventurous son?
Which ancestor left us
The ability to make sounds
        the gurgles, croaks,
        grunts, rasps, whistles;
        naming the birds,
        flowers, insects,
        animals of our territory?
Who taught us
To form languages: Chinese,
Persian, Navajo, Finnish?
Before the Tower of Babel
Could we all understand
Each other?
Was peony the same
The world over?
Was cat a cat wherever
You traveled?
Before there was Sanskrit,
Hebrew, Egyptian, Hittite,
Was there one sound
For the sound of men/women?
Did our ancestor feel compelled
To reproduce
The sounds of ocean waves,
        hums of bees,
        howls of coyotes,
        screeches of owls,
        wind brushing leaves...

Was the sound of the human voice
So loved that the ancestor
Experimented with the sounds
       of slender horns,
       bamboo flutes,
       strings on harps,
       hide drums?
When did the sounds become jazz,
       opera,
       rock 'n roll,
       concertos,
       heavy metal,
       folk music,
       chamber music,
       blues,
       rap?
Maybe it started with rap.

Turquoise Warrior
(for Scott)

"If my son had only been a bear..."*
...but he wasn't he was a
   large
    chunk
      of turquoise   uncut   awkwardly shaped

blue to the eyes   sacred to the ground

he was awed
  by a church   built of mud
knelt with respect   in the dust

he feels smooth
   as cool   as rock   cooled for
             a million years
after pitched
        from a sun

my son the large chunk of turquoise
dreams me as I dream him   we meet and part,
meet again   our words tumbling like creek rushing

water over turquoise   over smooth ragged stones
turquoise with light   no heat in its interior
my son the turquoise   chunk of warrior
   not a bear this time

this time   a dreaming warrior of a turquoise stone
uncut   not set on a silver necklace
   or a curving   belt of hide   uncut
standing
   alone
      dreaming   a warrior

* Garcia Lorca

Crumbling Adobe

The keeper of the gate at the ruins
leaned out of his booth.
The depth of his eyes
made us stop in the rocky heat,
the only visitors of the morning.
The keeper of the gate,
his face serious as the history
of his tribe,
leaned his square body toward us,
slow cadence of story-teller voice,
holding us in the eye of spiraling time,
ground deep voice chanting,
"The old ones lived here. You can hear
their voices in the silence.
Our people wandered from the old ways,
lost their power. The old ones warned
us that it would happen."
A jack rabbit dashed through the sage,
startled by an invisible movement.
In solemn silence
the keeper of the gate watched it flee
among pottery sherds, crumbling adobe...

When Butterflies Sing

I'll tell you why butterflies
  don't sing
  don't cry
  don't break their
    silence.

They fell under an enchantment
Millennia ago,
Were made voiceless
Only allowed to be beautiful
To float about
Flirting with golden wings,

Sometimes caught in nets,
Pinned to display boards
In silence.
No protest?
No cries in the night?

A wizard hid their voices
Inside a lacquered box
But they've seen anger,
Heard laughter,
They'll have a story to tell
When their silence is broken.

There's a magic rhyme
That breaks the spell.
They search for it.
They flutter the world
Looking for it.

They'll have a song
    to sing;
They will surely have
    a scream.
The time is upon us.

 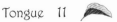

Winter Song

"Sometimes the dogs don't hear me..."
...but I sing a winter's song,
a song of snowflakes,
frost, and blonde men
with blue eyes that chill.

My song is the bark
of pine trees, lyrics
are the sap. I sing
of blizzards, dead men,

and the sky, white
with falling stars.
The pond is iced, I sing,
I've fallen deep

into darkness, cold
has swallowed my soul,
ink of black water
covers my heart, I sing

and rise in the morning
when the sun silvers icicles
that hang like chimes
from pine trees.

The dogs bark through
my songs, punctuate crisp air.
Their paw prints indent
the forest trail.

I follow them, singing
as I go, gathering snowflakes
as I go, singing winter, chilling
eyes, and cold.

The dogs don't hear me.

* Gerald Stern

All The Sea Knows

the red dogs on the gray deck
of the beach house
aren't talking

the sea is never silent
what the sea says, I say
the sea says it first

but I repeat the rhyme
I'd like to know
all the sea knows

all it knows
from the beginning of time
from every shore it's lapped

from every island it's touched
and run from
at the beach house

the red dogs lie quietly
but the sea rumbles
is never silent

if I listen deeply
in the star-embroidered night
the sea will fill me

and what it says, I'll say

I Missed It The First Time

You spoke to me
there on the dark path
among strong trees,
delicate shrubs,
in the mist rising
from waterfall.

What were you saying
about love,
about the heart
and its opening?
Your voice filled
my senses
but the words . . .

I thought I was listening.
I could hear song
of mockingbirds,
breath of butterflies,
burrowing of earthworms
but what was there about love
that you wanted me to know?

On another day when time
corkscrews into night,
and, once again, I wait
on the overgrown path,
listen for the voice
clearer than falling water,
louder than bird song,
butterfly breath,
burrowing earthworm . . .

I hope I won't be too late
to hear and understand.

Numinous

Poets believe in magic, wrap their spirits
in a cloak of skin, open their red hibiscus
hearts. They hear the stories of slain wolves,
hear voices of ancestors during Obon festivals.
Those unfolded stories, those oboe voices,
hover near poets, clamor to be incarnate.

Poets watch rainbows to feel how to dream,
hear the voices of Athabascan children,
Japanese grandfathers, Appalachian sisters.
Catch rivers of myth flowing through time,
carry the tales through the mist of waterfall:
the ceremonies of becoming, the way
to catch a shark, the piecing of quilts,
the honoring of crow and badger.

Poets dwell in other realms, have a sense
of enchantment. They marry a frog
to a princess, declare that a tree can rhyme.
They travel into space, bring back images
from suns where rocks talk and ashes dance.
Ghosts of horses visit them in their cars
as they drive along highways. Disembodied
wolves and panthers lie panting
under their beds, lending their strengths
to dream and illusion.

Native Dancers

If the indigenous people
Of America had conquered
The Europeans who came

To America's bays and harbors,
Our pale faces might be dancing
In the center of a circle,

Wearing long skirts, dancing
The clogging steps of Ireland
Or the round dances of middle Europe,

While the Hopi, Navajo, Arapaho, Apache,
Clap for us, give us money, ask rude
Questions about our ancient cultures.

We might slip back, then, into working clothes,
Sweep their hogan floors, dig their wells,
Cook their meals, mend their harness,

Groom their horses,
Whisper to ourselves stories and legends
Of our ancient heroes and artists:

    Shakespeare   Aristotle   Rembrandt
    Jesus   King George   Catherine of Aragon.

When we dance, we touch our past and ignore
The brown, dark-eyed faces encircling us,
Holding power over our public lives,

No power
Over our past, our memories, our pride.

Whatever They Say Must Be True

I don't know how many hairs a cat has
or how many tourists visit Tabrisi.
I don't know how many drops of paint
Rembrandt used in his lifetime.
No one else knows either
but we call ourselves educated.

Christopher Columbus was born in 1451,
they say, and they can point
to his stone house.
He studied maritime arts, though his father
was a weaver. They say Ludwig Von Beethoven
had a drunken father and a bad temper,
they say the aristocracy supported his genius
but his romantic loves were unrequited.
I don't know if it's true but it's what they say.

My friend Elaine says the best slot machine
to play is one at the end of a row. Janet
says the best ones are near the entrance
of the casino. I don't know. I didn't win
after trying both.

I heard that on the coastal hills by Pacifica
there is a place where lie bones of original
Americans and pottery sherds — washed free
by rain and wind. I don't know.
I wanted to pay my respects and looked
but never found the right place.

I don't know where tamarinds grow,
I've never seen them. Whether they're juicy
or dry, orange or crimson, is something
I've not experienced.
I don't know if cinnamon grows in Ceylon
or if tea grows in Assam
because I've never visited either place.
I only know what they say.

Where Demons Tremble

"Let us go and make our visit..."
where the mad must make their homes
and not fear their unexpected turn
of phrase, their visions, starkly vivid
in the darkness of their nights

let us listen to their voices, clicking,
clacking through their tongues
waltz with them where demons tremble
hear them sing and chant to keep from harm

their delicate embraces lead us down
the electric path where lightning
is the key, the password, startling
us to jerk and twist and bend the knee

let us go and make a visit
though the welcome mat's not out
there are memories to master
there are senses hidden deep

barely tasted in the murky realms of sleep
walk the pathways, hand outstretched,
offer all your kind attention
nothing less will give them peace

* T.S. Eliot

Eyes Of Knowing

you look
into the face
of a stranger
and he knows
who you are

knows
to the deep sea
of you
salty blood
surf-grass nerves
conch-coil brain
and more

knows
the grief
that resounds
to andantes
of cellos
the joy that rocks
to staccato piano
the characters
you have played
as you've twisted
through space
and time

you look
at a stranger
who shocks
through the eyes
of his knowing
who whispers
your secret
name

II. Raspberries

Raspberries — A Ghazal

The vines in the backyard of my Oregon house
were in even rows.
The home owner prior to me had planted, then staked, the
raspberries.

The wedding dinner was sumptuous and filling.
The most delicate and pleasing course was a sweet ice of
raspberries.

There are places in the world that are too hot, too dry.
Children starve there, will never know the brilliance of
sour/sweet raspberries.

On Air Force One the President, wearing his most expensive
black suit, reads and prepares a formal speech.
In the President's right hand, red juice dripping, is a popsicle of
raspberry.

Constance, what does that red tartness mean to you?
What memories are evoked by the velvet of raspberries?

Wading in creek beds in the summer, children grow hungry.
They scatter to forest's edge, searching, not for truth but for
the dignity of raspberries.

Lovers sipping Champagne watch the play of lights
on city skyline, make solemn vows.
They sip again the bubbling wine, find an unexpected flavor on
their tongues, a lingering of raspberry

It Was Summer

That year we wore our dads' white
shirts that fell just above our knees
and just below our teen-aged pudenda.

My best friend told me of her summer
romance in Cotati, an older boy
who shaved, who brashed her delicate

skin with his beard's shadow.
We sat among blue lupines on a cliff
above the Pacific and she told me

of his tongue pushing thickly, wetly
into her willing mouth. I ignored the stains
accumulating on my dad's white shirt

as I rolled over and over among the deep
blue lavender of lupines. She described
how, in the movie balcony, he unbuttoned

her dad's white shirt, stroked her newly formed
breasts, one, then the other, how her shirt
wrinkled from their sweat, one button falling

to the midnight of the floor. That tiny
white button, falling. I plucked flowers
as I listened, making a lupine garland.

I did not know the touch of a tongue,
slippery in my mouth, the feel of boyfingers
twisting my nipples. I was repulsed

at the intrusion of my friend's body
by a stranger-boy, felt my own body threatened
by sweat and saliva in darkness, vowed

I would never let a boy touch me
with tongue and fingers…
felt my body beneath the white shirt

tremble with desire for the touch.

A Purple Experience

Lick a purple rose
Does it taste
As sweet as love? Do the red thorns
Make your tongue
Bleed like rejection? Throw it away.
It was only an experience.

Lying Alone In A Cotton Slip . . .

the heat so fierce my skin is burning,
oozing moisture, my hair lies limply
on the white pillow.

Downstairs are my aunts, uncles, cousins.
They would make me welcome if I left
this attic, joined them around the table

or on the orange front-porch swing.
I would rather be swatted like a June bug,
feel my shell crunch under the blow.

Not for me the taste of vanilla ice cream
with chunks of peaches, hand-churned
by the family's youngest.

No, I'm the strange one in the attic, lying
in my white cotton slip, drafting poems
my family won't read. If I glided down

the twenty attic steps, they would embrace me,
call my name, offer me iced tea, Red Velvet cake
but I can't walk down those worn wooden

steps. It is too hot,
I am only wearing a slip
and why is it that no one climbs up to me?

It Wasn't Rapunzel

I dream of a Princess in a tower, its walls painted
with moons, stars, planets. Flowers and vines twine
abundantly around its base. The Princess is regal,
swathed in robes of pink and gold, hair covered
by snowy linen, brow topped by a jeweled crown
of gold. She languishes, she waits. Surrounded
by beauty but nowhere to go.

Here flies her rescuer, a noble Prince, astride
a roan horse, a magic horse that leaps above
the earth, suspends itself near the tower top.
The Prince tongue-kisses the trapped Princess.
The world belongs to him. He flies over it
with his magical steed, allows the wind to caress
his hair. He sets down wheresoever he pleases.

The Princess whispers in her hero's ear, giggles,
crooks a delicate finger. The horse prances
on a cloud while the Prince loosely ties its reins
over a carved railing by the open window.
The man joins the woman in the tower top.
He spins twice in a frenzy, throws off his cloak,
heavy with gold and silver embroidery, stands

with arms out-thrown in his inner garments
of blue silk. The Princess snatches up
the embroidered cloak, throws it over her shoulders,
is out of the tower and astride the fine-muscled horse
with the speed of a hummingbird. She gathers the reins,
sings to the Prince, "Wait patiently and in time a Princess
may come to rescue you."

With a cheerful flip of the reins she rides full gallop
across the evening sky, head spinning with the pent-
up energy of ten thousand years of imprisonment.
She'll find a whirlwind and tame it while the Prince
remains in his prison tower, sighing at the moon,
writing poetry, waiting to be freed by a lovely Princess.

Scabby Knees And Make-up

Down at the branch
We loved the feel
Of rich brown mud
Squelching between bare toes.

We sat in the middle
Of slow-flowing summer water,
Piled mud over legs,
Faces, arms
"Doing a mud pack," we said,
Hoping to improve
Our complexions.

Growing bored,
My sister, cousins and I
Ran across the pasture,
Avoiding cow plops,
Dangerous cows,
To the leaning barn,
Climbed up the inside ladder
To play in the hayloft.

We piled square hay bundles
Into walls to form
Rooms for our house,
Earnestly began testing
Avon make-up samples
Stolen from Aunt Norine's
Demonstration pack.

So glamorous, we felt,
Up there in the hay loft,
With our denim shorts,
Scabby knees, bare feet,
Faces adorned
With red, pink and blue,
Ears and flat bosoms
Scented with
Apple, gardenia, jasmine.

Silk Stockings — 1945

The black seams
Up the back
Were never straight.
You could only
Purchase them
With a ration coupon.
At the slightest
Puncture they ran
A ladder pattern
Up your shaved leg.
If the run
Started above the hemline, You could use
Carnelian Red nail polish
To stop it.
Below the hemline,
You had to use Clear.
It caked on your skin,
Peeled off
When you took off
Your stocking.
You held them up
With garters —
Cloth-covered rubber bands —
Which cut into your thighs,
Rolled the tops
Of the silky stockings
Around the elastic garter.
If you were sophisticated,
You wore an embroidered
Garter belt with tabs of metal and elastic,
Creating a lump
Beneath a thin dress and slip.
You always, always wore a slip.
So no one could see
Where your silk-clad legs
Divided

Not In Downtown Manhattan

a certain smile, elegantly erotic
a floor polished for dancing

tables draped with white lace
fracture of violins
shimmer of rose candlesticks

I'm sorry, I don't dance well

your voice both tough and edgy
shoulders spontaneous as spring

I struggle against the feeling,
the corrosive effect of clutching
secrets

I'm sorry I don't dance well

a search
for passion in the dimness

my profound sense of dislocation —
   twists and whispers of tangos
      show me that life

is shaped by desire

I don't dance well, I'm sorry

my only consolation is the fusion
   of intelligence with the sensual

and a delicious romp through lanes
   lined by rain-swollen lilacs, unfortunately,
      not in downtown Manhattan

love is an inexplicable act of provocation
   in the center of ordinary life

I long to embrace you
but I don't dance well

Race Ya'

"*A particularly seductive stable boy...*"*
riding a low-slung white convertible,
his left arm casually hooked
over the door frame —
I edged past him on the freeway,
then slowed, noticing his tan,
his Florida license plate,
his cocky smile as he saw me
racing by his side at seventy miles
an hour, saw me looking at him,
couldn't know I was thinking,
"Oh, to be twenty years younger,
I'd race you to the nearest off-ramp,
the nearest Motel 6, spend an afternoon
within a closed-blind room
on white cotton sheets, ruffle
your hair the way the wind
is ruffling it now."
But being over fifty,
on my way to work, too broke
for even a Motel 6, I ease my foot
off the accelerator, let him fly
past me. I don't bother to smile.

* Virginia Woolf

III. Rain

Rain — A Ghazal

Among the emerald shoots of tulips, a dead branch has fallen.
It is sheltering ants and snails from a fierce winter rain.

In Maine the Republican Presidential candidates are debating.
They stand inside halls at podiums, sheltered from the rain.

Last year I kissed my dying sister goodbye, as her eyes looked
at me with kindness.
Behind her bed the window was blessed with winter's first
showers of rain.

Put out suet cakes for insect eaters this winter.
Insects that form meals-on-wings for birds are grounded
by the rain.

Constance, be careful how you speak of secret things.
Your whisperings fall on the green grass like silent rain.

The last of the summer's scarlet roses are clinging
to their bush.
A poet ponders their brief lives, staring through the
downpour of rain.

Earthquake epicenters are far away but the fault lines run
under my house.
Every year the walls crack a little more, allow in more soft
flutters of rain.

Autumn Storm

Wind whipping trees on canyon top,
a whoosh of grand sound, even hawks
fold their wings, shelter against rock.

I grip the car wheel, slide along wet
pavement on high Taos mesa, below me
in canyon floor two wild rivers converge,

headed, like me, for Santa Fe.

The wild rivers continue on to Mexico,
Soon I'll settle on one haunch on a couch
inside a faux adobe house, a couch

as purple black as the mesa at midnight.
I'll remember wild rivers, whoosh
of tree branches in autumn storm,

abuse my liver with mellow malt
whiskey, write a poem to the beat
of a drum played with my toes,

write five hundred poems by tomorrow,
when I get bored, soar over canyon walls
with wings spread.

Golden Shroud

I wandered off a cliff
    one rainy night,
Found I could   float
In the air
    like an angel,

Found wings   sprouting
    from my shoulders,
As the rain
    pelted down,
Dampened my white   feathers.

Below me,
    waters tumbled and boiled
        along the canyon floor

Illuminated   by lightning ribbons.

I grasped a ribbon,
    wound it around me,
    like a golden   shroud,
Enclosed my   wings,

Plummeted to the bottom
    of the canyon

    Spiraled into
       the center
        of the
           molten
             earth.

The Diviner

In a desert shaded by evening, a diviner,
carrying a two-pronged stick, seeks water,
an underground river of healing for a parched

land. Seeks to pull life to the surface,
for flowering orchids of purple and white,
for date palms, almond groves, shrubs

of cinnamon and tea. Enticing moisture
and vapor to feed the breath, bring
to the surface a river that now roils

and rages beneath the sand; the source of myth
and dream aroused. The diviner walks barefoot
across hot sands, holds willow-wood

laced with green lichen. The air is still,
no wind billows her white robe. The stick,
outstretched in delicate hands, bends tensely

toward the river's magnet. The diviner chants,
"Here are the waters of poetry, of life,
of healing." She scoops a bowl in the sand

using her hands in the repetitive rhythms
of childbirth, drum beat, pulsing of blood.
The hollow fills with water — clear, sweet

as golden melons. It spreads, deepens. The woman
drops her garment, bathes in the river flowing
around her, river pouring forth over barren
desert.

Rainy Cold Day In Oakland

I'd like to travel down under,
feel the breeze of a kangaroo's leap,
see her black against a round red sun,

like to peer down into a pink
diamond mine at Argyle,
smell the sharp aroma of diamond

dust, see the sweat glow on a miner's
dark back, walk a wooden sidewalk
watching for unexpected excitement.

If I ran into you quaffing a warm pint
at a worn down pub, looking fine
as the day I married you, I'd pass

you by, wouldn't blow a kiss, pat
your fanny, or shake your hand.
I'd grab a feisty fellow wearing

a broad-brimmed hat, a sweat-stained
scarf around his neck, whisper in his ear
that I come from a cooler climate

but I can take the heat. Walk on out
with my Australian truck driver,
leave you sitting, quaffing.

I'd go down the road a piece in the dusty
truck with the driver's hand crawling
up my skirt and if his touch was hot

I might stay awhile, buy a mine of pink
diamonds, quaff a few warm beers,
learn to love a hot, hot touch.

Behind The Window

*"Cars sleeping at the curb..."**
...and at Days Inn across the street
orange neon lights illuminate
the wet dark pavement

and sleeping cars. At 4 a.m.
streets are nearly empty
of moving vehicles, an occasional

early riser squishes by,
rubber against fallen rain.
Standing at the window with curtain

pulled back, early morning is lonely,
as if the sun had shifted, leaving
few alive in the darkness.

Now, it is not raining, only water
trembling through a gutter
and slick road reflecting street lights,

motel neon, prove that recently
ten thousand drops of rain fell
from blackened skies.

Behind the window I watch 4 a.m.
loneliness, searching for a reason for continuing
to wait for the sun that may

have shifted while I slept.

* Naomi Shihab-Nye

Taste Of Sun

Mangoes and oranges, a hit parade
of fruit   gathering of sun
to brighten a sunless
day   it rains
          it blows
what is it
  that rains
    that blows?

a goddess's teary eyes?
  a god's angry breath?

Juice of fruit spilling
from mouth corners, brilliant taste
of sun on a day of clouds

I see ghosts of friends adrift in the currents
beyond the window   it rains   it blows

what is it that rains   that blows?

low pressure from Japan, from the Steppes
of Mongolia   a system   designed by what?

it rains   it blows

    ghosts are singing but the words are too faint
to be heard   over the rain   the blowing wind

a mango of rain
  an orange of blowing wind
juice in the corners of ghosts' mouths

and then the sun
  what is it
      the sun?

There Must Be Something
That Has Never Been Formed Into A Song

I long for the space of a river
Overhung with giant purple trees
That have escaped
The world's attention.
Let me describe
The veins in the leaves
That when severed
Leak lavender ambrosia.
Let me float on that piece
Of river, watch turtles
Nesting in trees.

Let me hear the call
of an Egyptian desert bird
With silky green beard,
Singing a melody
Not yet recorded.
Let me be in that moon-lit
Desert when the night bird trills.

If a miniature elephant
With yellow spots
On the coast of India,
Playfully squirts a nose
Full of water to cool
Me off, let me feel it
On my hot skin,
Write the lyrics with scarlet ink.

Let me be
Fully present
Let me   See.

IV. Shadow

Shadow — A Ghazal

In my dream I cannot see your face.
You stand in the shade of shadows.

The black sea, the surf, lies behind the fog.
The coast road is a winding shadow.

A white mask of linen covers the player's expression.
The stage is full of silvery shadows.

At dusk the redwood tree is a colorless silhouette.
On the balcony the geraniums are gray as shadows.

Constance, what do you think is hidden?
What lies behind your mother's shadow?

A siren in the distance urges cars to the side of the road.
In the ambulance rides a presence composed of shadow.

The sun bursts over the eastern horizon.
Children, dashing to school, chase their shadows.

Linked Baskets

I linger in a dim Berkeley shop piled with heaps
of woven baskets. Visions of skilled feminine
hands around the world tremble in the air.

Nimble fingers wove these patterns with grass,
leaf fronds, softened canes. Soft colors stain
these reeds, vegetable dyes; muted hues of deserts.

A Hopi tightly wove this grain basket to hold
life-giving seed, these geometric designs transmitted
through grandmothers for generations.

I stroke a lacquered red-stained wedding basket
from China once filled with bridal sweets.
Each incomparable shape weaves a magic story,

racial memories. Scents of rich soil, fragrant woods,
dried rushes are the primal essence of each form.
Touching a basket, I am linked with women sitting

on the earth in Africa, Asia, the Americas,
    selecting slim reeds,
        weaving us into one people.

Dreaming Of Snakes

A circular serpent, a coiled dreamer
of a serpent, an emerald-eyed, narrow-
eyed, diamond-backed serpent that lies
under a dreamer's bed, sheds the truth
as readily as skin.

Dreams for hire, dreams of fire, of fate,
of circular tales from a genie's lamp,
a true dream of a circle, of a crash
of cars along a sea wall, an uncrushed
hand with a ring of emerald-eyed serpents.

A tale of Vienna, of a poet, a dreamer
denying dreams, laughing at the dreams
behind reality, a circle of poems,
a mandala of coiled serpents, tales
of a dream writer who dreamed

her passage through a tunnel,
of the comfort at the end, of basking
in dreamlight, the foretelling,
the forbidden knowledge of apples,
serpents, emeralds, the tunnels of dreams,

a richly woven tale, a remnant of ancient
tapestry, caught beneath a basket
of sweet rushes, a coiled basket filled
with apples, emerald-eyed serpents,
a bushel of fate, a gathering of eyes,

no ending to the tale but a serpent,
its tail caught in its mouth, a hoop
of life.

Mandala's Eye

The opening to my city
Under the sea
Is through the eye
Of the Mandala,
The rhythm is the beat
Of surf rushing
Against continent's edge.
Dance with it
Through the black and white
Doorway. Take your songs
With you.

Anemone blossoms
Float with the current,
Their roots buried in the sand
Of fluid sea mountains.
Sea horses prance maneless
Among the scarlet flowers.
Playful women are at the heart,
The center, of ebb and flow.
They cause bronze bells to chime
Throughout the watery Queendom,
Tolling their poems.

No children cry in pain
In the sea city.
No flowers are outraged.
No animals gallop in fear.
Weapons, buried in mud
Are homes for barnacles.
We dwell in abandoned seashells
Of peach and cream
At the center of the sea.
You may enter at the doorway
Of the Mandala's eye.

Vanishing Point

The hallway linoleum is slick from yellowed wax,
from footsteps. At the entrance one cannot see
the exit, it is far away, the hallway narrows
to darkness. On each side of the slick linoleum
pathway are doors painted pink, beige, red, gray.
They are blank with no distinction but color.
The game is that one must enter a certain number

of doors, progressing through the hallway, in
and out of doorways, until one reaches the exit.
No going back. No hightailing it back to the entrance.
No going through a portal more than once. One
knows the rules, though they are not spoken
aloud. They are not written on parchment, typed
in ink. The rules are the same for each one

passing through the corridor. No one remembers
if the rules were known before entering the hallway
but when one is there, ready to choose the first door,
the rules are clear. There are decisions to make.
Choose a door on the left or the right. The pink
or the beige. Does it matter? Should one run quickly
from door to door — in/out —

in/out — or pace majestically, slowly, from one
door to the other? Should each be opened
or should one walk past six and open the seventh?
Sooner or later one chooses. The journey begins,
the corridor shortens, the door at the end,
the last door, the tangerine door, begins
to be visible, to glow. As one moves in and out,

along the slick yellowed hallway, the doors become
fewer and fewer. One knows that the tangerine
exit is drawing closer. Only three or four choices
remain. The rules are: No turning back,
no going through any door twice, all decisions
have been made and are final. Only the tangerine
door. . .go on through!

My Sister's Cancer Is Back

After surgery, chemo, nausea,
gut-wrenching pain; after losing
all body hair, growing it again,

the cancer is back.
This time she is more frightened,
understanding exactly what she faces.

I think of this every day.
Not constantly, but from time to time
and know that she, too, thinks of it.

Even when she is laughing,
her voice slides high with fear.
She tries not to notice what lies ahead

but when I wake in the night,
I know that she lies in her bed thinking
of her children and grandchildren,

her husband, mother, sisters, brother.
Knowing that they are hurting for her
is extra pain to bear, having to tell

them all, yes, the cancer is back, yes,
more surgery, yes, more chemo.
We shrug and laugh with her and say,

"Oh, well, one day at a time, we're all
headed for the same door." The whole
family wonders why this pain exists

for the best of us, the most gentle,
the most self sacrificing. She just says,
"Well, why not me?"

Morning Of The Red Mist

"Throw open the shutter..."*
...let the clouds rush in, smother
the room in a red mist tinted
by the morning sun.

Downstairs bacon sizzles,
oatmeal bubbles. I knew life
was too good and that a red mist

must be coming. It covers the white
spread on the bed, merges into the red
and white of cheerful cotton rugs.

It is creeping up my ankles. I think
that it must be hot and will burn
but it merely numbs. Downstairs

the radio is playing a Patti Loveless
tune, "...a man is a Stetson hat..."
The shutters are open, the clouds

are here, touching my hair, while
in the kitchen toast is browning,
coffee is sending its morning aroma.

I'd hoped for more sunshine days,
maybe a year or two, but this morning
I threw open the shutters and in rushed

   clouds   of red mist

* Rita Dove

Where Van Gogh Paints

"Put your ear down to your soul
*and listen hard.**
There's silence and color
In the tunnel
And you can't escape
And it goes on forever
Sufis dance there
Broadway shows play there
Krishna is blue there
There is no there
Keep looking
Go deeper
The tunnel is a black
Cyclone
Terrifying and intense
Van Gogh paints there
Anne Sexton writes poems there
They couldn't find their way out
Buddha did
Called it Nirvana
Snails shielded his head
From the sun
When he sat

* Anne Sexton

In The Course Of My Duties...

1. I made an appointment
    to visit a woman
    in a nursing home.
    I entered her room
    to discover
    she was a corpse,
    lying on a gurney
    placed next to her bed,
    her head and shoulders
    wrapped in clear plastic,
    her legs naked and waxy
    as tallow candles.

2. On Thanksgiving Day
    my sister sat quietly
    in a big chair, watching
    her grandchildren, her
    great nieces, playing.
    She was carefully dressed
    and made up, her wig
    on straight.
    She responded to questions,
    smiled at the children,
    volunteered nothing.
    She should have been
    in a hospital bed
    but was determined
    not to spoil the holiday.
    When we say goodbye,
    I hug her and kiss
    her cheek, then draw
    away in surprise.
    It is as cold and waxy
    as a tallow candle.

Weep, Lonely Pine Tree

the house stands deserted
window panes broken
chimney bricks crumbling

weep, lonely pine tree

the parents have died
children departed
wild roses climb over the door

are you watching, lonely pine tree

sons have been wounded in war
daughters have been abandoned
tree branches shadow the house

keep vigil, lonely pine tree

once laughter and love smiled within
work was hard but a joy
fields grew thick with green corn

stand silent, lonely pine tree

dreams still linger in corners
ghosts drift in during storms
voices have long been silenced

weep, lonely pine tree

Standing Alone On A Lofty Ridge

(From a painting by Gao Qipei)

Breezes blow my blue and white robe.
The sun is setting in the Western sky.
My grown children have tossed me out,

claiming that I, their father, empty
the wine jug far too frequently.
All day I have climbed up this mountain,

have no strength to climb down.
My children say I reek of sour wine,
curse and strike out when I am drunk.

Breezes are strong here and cold.
I am an old man, weak, slightly drunk.
My wine jug, a gift from my own father,

is empty once again.
The only path from this lofty
ridge is the path of a eagle,

riding air currents, plunging for prey.
When I fail to return, my children
will gather my broken bones

from the valley floor below me, burn them,
carry an ash-filled urn back
to the home from which I departed

before sunrise.

Go Tell

to be dead a long time, to be lonely
tell it to the flowers
listen to the breath of pine trees

the dead are alone
daffodils and narcissus keep watch
let the pine trees whisper to you

tell it to the flowers
say it is lonely here
under the pine trees

say their needles cover me,
warm me but still …
flowers and loneliness

pine trees
  and silence
    tell the flowers

V. Light

Light — A Ghazal

There's a dancing goat in my dream.
Its pointy beard is pale as morning light.

I laughed and laughed when my little sister, jumping
with joy, lifted both feet from the floor at once
and fell on her ass. She should have floated in the air
like motes of light.

Pouring water from a watering can into a bed of tulips,
a rainbow forms.
What joy to the eye, those shades of pure light.

The player postures and shouts on the shadowy stage.
Her body outlined by a red nimbus of light.

Constance, don't fear the dark.
Trust that there will always be someone to guide you
back to the warm and glowing light.

A careless man presses too hard on the gas pedal, driving
a winding country road.
Suddenly, before him is a doe, trapped in his headlights.

Somesay that ignorance is bliss.
Somesay it is an abyss, an absence of light.

A Chair Of Sturdy Pine

a pine of a chair, a paint peeling,
peeling blue, peeling white, green,
sturdily standing in a cabin of hickory logs,
logs peeled of bark, peeled of sap,
dried under Carolina sun, sunnily warm
and dried, naked and peeled,
peeled as the pine chair, the rungs
of the chair, the slats, the seat,
the rounds of the legs, not painted,
only scraps of paint remaining
on bare pine, shaved, hammered,
sanded pieces of pine, holding seats,
bone-skinny seats, seats of pine,
seats with resin dried in the seams,
sun dried, heat of bodies dried,
the bare sturdy chair, the peeling
paint on the chair, stripped of years
of paint, one coat of white, one coat
of green, one of turquoise, of cream,
one hundred years of painted, peeling
pine, from rooted pines, evergreen
pines, Carolina pines, the fruit
of red earth, fruit of skilled hands,
hands sanding pine planks, planks
of wood, rounds of wood, the breath
and scent of pine wood, the knots
of pine, whorls of pine, pine standing
in forests, in mountains, near springs,
pines shading white-flag deer, holding
mocking birds, pines standing tall, pines
falling, falling for planks, for chairs.

Approach Of The White Fox

("The moon gnaws your left side.")*

The moon found me on the frozen tundra.
It gnaws my left side, like a yellow bear,
leaving a hole filled with blood and the torn

ends of veins and capillaries. It gnaws
my left side because I'm lying on my right
and the sky is orange. A white fox approaches,

cautiously, afraid that the moon, hanging
like a wide round Chinese lantern
in the orange sky will grip his left side

with teeth the shape of small mountains.
I watch the white fox approach but know
she won't save me. She is part of this waking

dream and there is menace in her pace,
despite the purity of her white winter coat.
I see the orange sky reflected in her eyes

as they watch me. Our gazes touch
but there is no struggle. She draws me easily
into her body as my own body deadens

into an arctic block. I become the cautious
fox. I can feel her blood pumping warmly,
see the moon, the ice, the orange sky

through eyes that feel strange, vision distorted.
I, the fox, begin to run, pads moving swiftly
away from the gnawing yellow bear of a moon,

seeking a den, a place to hide until the moon
    is driven away by the sun's brilliance.

* Marilyn Chin

Habit Of The Night

I'm the night with wolves pacing
I'm the night where ghosts hover
I'm the night filled with black trees
    open-eyed barn owls
    sleeping red-tailed hawks

I'm the night with soldiers crawling
I'm the night where women cry
I'm the night where babes suckle
    horses sigh
    mule deer wrestle
    panthers prey

I'm the night with telescopes seeking
    search lights turning
    police sirens screaming
I'm the night where burglars search
    where call girls hurt
    where suicides call
I'm the night with empty streets
    shadowed alleys
    neoned boulevards

I pull light out of the sky
        sun from its heaven
I'm the habit of the night
        dream of the night
        law of the night
I'm the night found in Kivas
        sounded by gongs
        foretold by sibyls

I'm the night heard in Wagner
        the night that can't be seen
        the night stroked by velvet fingers
        lapped by thrusting tongues
I'm the night that catches dreams
        hides fear
        is the oracle of pleasure
I'm the night   feel me around you
        touching your skin   taste me
        hear me   know me

Fool's Day

Wild goose moon
in a Fool's Day sky,
a solitary goose hanging there,
left the rest of the gaggle,
left them flying behind.
They couldn't catch her wildness.
She landed on the moon,
absorbed it, soars white in the black
sky, no fool, she.

Reflections

One by one they came,
always dancing tango,
you don't have to be a tribal
person to know the bird
is a mirror

It became too hot
to stay inside my skin
I became dried lavender flowers

Minerva, patroness of poets and artists,
placed a few white blossoms
next to a fragrant spring
the spring is also a mirror

Toss your guilt
into the breeze
the wind is all encompassing

Puzzle Pieces

Genius and its difficulties

        don't mean I shall walk

    with my back straight in art
        museums of crowded alligators,

painted faces,   turquoise snakes.

        In the circular world of newspaper
ribbons,
        the road uncurls before me,
   yes,
        obvious,
            something anyone
would have done and any one element

of the. . .Right! I used to be John
    Lennon with full moon round face,

eating crab and I was quiet. She

                    told me off, let me feel it
              on my hot skin. The multiple
        physical tabs in a book
                 are visible all at once

                       in little Japanese cookies,

caramel
   corn
      seaweed
         crackers.

      It kind of made me want to cry,

   the fragility of small things.

It's Me! Emma Goldberg

To my doctors and nurses
I'm a patient.
My blood pressure is too high
My legs are too weak
My toenails are mycotic
My brain is an organic syndrome
   of dementia.
No, it isn't true!   It's me!
Emma Goldberg.

To my lawyer and his paralegal
I'm a client.
My phone calls are too frequent
My Will needs a codicil
My doctor must be sued
My son fled to Mexico with
   my savings.
No, it isn't true!   It's me!
Emma Goldberg.

To the Judge and the Court Investigator
I'm a conservatee.
My rights must be protected
My attendance at Court is required
My daughter will handle my affairs
My residence and medical treatment
    decided by others.
No, it isn't true!   It's me!
Emma Goldberg.

It's me, Emma Goldberg:
I teach physics to Freshmen
I'm beautiful and charming
I love poetry and music
I dance light as air with
    handsome men.
Yes, it's true!
Do you see me?   It's me!
Emma Goldberg.

Backing Into The Light

It's emptiness you bump against when very ill,
maybe dying. Dying is right there waiting,

a firm black wall. . .no scents, colors, scenes, tastes. . .
Emptiness you stumble into. If you manage to back

away, light and color return, scent of pink
rosebuds ring the room. You understand that you

are a hollow shell, a body and mind on the verge
of emptiness: to live is to fill the void. . .

As you back away from illness/death, you understand
that life is imaginary, created by you inch by inch

and you must create it again:
        A taste of hot creamy soup,
        A poem on a white page,
        A telephone call.

You sense the vigor necessary to build a life, moment
by transitory moment. . .Possessions are our props,

they surround us, hold us in our special place:
        That statue on the shelf
            I picked up in Chinatown when I worked there,

        That book in its bright red cover
           was given me by a friend,

        Those yellow chairs I chose
           because they looked like solid sunshine.

A Variety Of Angels

One angel who lives south of here
has wings of hot pink gauze,
no feathers at all.
An angel I spent a good bit
of time with carried a tambourine
and had translucent wings
in shades of amber and umber.

They all dwell in heavenly
places, have deep chuckles,
and always give
a human an outstretched hand.
Some have auras like little flames
above their heads, some a golden
disc banded in silver. An angel
who often lands in Alaska
has wings like white fur,
wears a halo of rainbow dust.

One sings to me when I'm sad,
one makes me laugh, if I take
myself seriously.
My favorite makes a Tibetan
sand painting by my bed each night
and blows it away before morning.

Feminine Eyes

your eyes do not
make mistakes
they see around
corners, behind
picture frames

taped to the wall
a picture of enormous
suns shining
on space-far planets
your eyes can see
that exact distance
they do not
make mistakes
no need to question

their ability, they see
three women in quilted
gowns with ermine collars
one deals Tarot cards
one sips black tea
one plays a lute
your eyes see them naked
see them exposed
to their souls
and they are fine
your eyes see
and do not
make mistakes

VI. Picture

Picture — A Ghazal

On a windy March morning, kites flown by children
dance and swoop.
One kite is a dragon, another a rabbit, on a third
has been pasted a child's picture.

The radio reports a six-car pile up, including a jack-knifed
semi on Albert Street.
Hovering overhead in a copter, a reporter for the evening
news takes picture after picture.

I visit a woman in a nursing home who chats cheerfully,
speaks of her husband as if he were still alive.
All that remains, though, is a memory and on her dresser,
her dead husband's picture.

A new head of the International Money Fund will be selected
soon.
A German is expected to get the job and in a long dark
hallway will hang his picture.

Images, Constance, flow through your mind, appearing
and disappearing.
A cessation of images is coming but it's not easy to picture.

Like exhaust from jet engines, gas and dust of the Nebula
M2-9 rush from a dying star at more than one hundred
miles a second.
The Hubble Space Telescope captures the picture.

Six children at a birthday party wear cone hats, play
ring around the rosy and drop the handkerchief.
The mother of the birthday child points a camera, opens
the shutter; a picture.

Ground Squirrels

I cleaned a cupboard this morning,
baked Anzac cookies, hosted
the Fresh Ink poets.
This afternoon I get my hair permed.
Last week I got new mini-blinds
for my study and bedroom.

For what am I organizing?
Readying my nest for winter?
Making ready to store my nuts
and grains for a cold, hard season?

The nuts are all in my head,
rattle around in there
when I shake my head to a Zydeco
beat. Yeah, I feel a little
squirrelly.

There's a squirrel
that climbs from her tree
to my balcony. Comes up
to the open door, puts her
two front paws up to her chest,
begging to come in or at least
get fed.

I tell her
there is only room
for one squirrel in this house

Yellow School Bus Graveyard

We discovered the yellow school bus graveyard,
While exploring the neighborhood,
One spring Saturday morning.

We hid and peeked from behind
Raggedy pine trees,
Saw no adults to shoo us.

Black letters, half concealed
By long grass, Queen Anne's Lace,
Kudzu vines spelled

NEWTON
NORTH CAROLINA
SCHOOL DISTRICT

Arguing, pushing and shoving,
We chose the best broken yellow bus
For Saturday morning play.

Together, we shifted heavy doors.
Jackie, Brenda and I stepped inside
A wheel-less, derelict, secret clubhouse.

We swept out dirt, sow bugs, June bugs,
Cobwebs and spiders; tore out rotten
Cotton stuffing down to wooden slats.

We cleared out the mess, fearing
Discovery by adults and bites from snakes,
Hiding in the kudzu or under bus seats.

By summer's end we had abandoned
The yellow school bus graveyard,
Having drawn out all satisfaction.

Taos Inn

A monk might have slept
In this room;
Adobe walls — whitewashed,
Peeled logs supporting
The ceiling,
Simple oak bedstead
With plainly carved
Headboard,
Straight end posts,
This as an ascetic life.

The gray woolen blanket
Striped
With golden brown and aqua,
Woven by a pueblo woman,
Would have kept him warm
In the coolness
Of the high desert night.

Opening the oak door
From outside the small
Cell, he would have
Stepped down over the rounded
Mud threshold
Into the windowless room,
Like stepping into a cave.
His light would have been
Softly flickering
Tallow candles.

No way to avoid knowing
Who you are
In a room like this,
No worldly distractions
To confuse you,
Just mud, wool, wood,
Your self.

Oldest Book Shop In New Mexico

Sitting on the loose-stone patio
Between the Cafe Taza and the Taos bookstore,
Writing poems, painting pictures.
Thunder clouds gather overhead.

Between the Cafe Taza and the Taos Bookstore
Orange-red peonies bow to purple and yellow pansies.
Thunder clouds gather overhead;
Sudden showers send the artists scattering.

Orange-red peonies bow to purple and yellow pansies,
Brighten the thick adobe walls.
Sudden showers send the artists scattering,
Blessing the dry earth with moisture.

Brighten the thick adobe walls,
Sheltering books full of desert tales.
Blessing the dry earth with moisture,
Goddesses send rain for seedlings.

Sheltering books full of desert tales,
The Taos bookstore holds treasures.
Goddesses send rain for seedlings,
To nourish the spirits of the artists,
Sitting on the loose-stone patio.

Chiles — Red Chiles

Seeing through a window in Taos:
mud walls with roof poles painted blue;
artists with slender brushes capturing
light, cloud, shadow; necklaces
of colored corn in every shop;
a roughly woven shawl of evening
shades of rose and blue.

Through a Taos window
no distortions
Red chiles — hot — hot
with flavor for beans, rice —
Cold mountain water for quenching,
for cooling chile pepper mouths,
round mouths from which flows
hot stories of original people,
seen clearly through a Taos window.

A dousing rod twitches
when it's found love,
love through a Taos window.
Keep watching for a wolf,
hoping for a bear,
hearing a raven call.
The moon warns through the window
pane of painful life
but soothes those who mud
the holy church, bow to blue
cornflowers, white morning glories.

Celebrate morning corn ceremony,
scatter meal in four directions,
plant a garden of beans,
tomatoes, corn, onions, eat
from earth's center, food
spiced with red chiles, seen
through a Taos window.

Jardín De Los Tres Mujeres

Hooked to the wire fence
a sign in Spanish
painted on a rough board
in blue letters claims
the garden at Las Casitas
for three women.

> *Black-cloaked nuns once lived*
> *in the adobe cells of Las Casitas;*
> *planted lettuce, corn, peas,*
> *taught children*
> *in the shadow of the white cross*
> *at the Church*
> *Of Our Lady of Guadalupe.*

The garden is protected
by a fence of chicken wire
and split logs, as irregular,
as if built by children.

> *The Virgin, appearing to an Indian boy*
> *in Guadalupe, Mexico, caused red roses*
> *to grow in barren rock, their color*
> *and fragrance blessing the desert.*

Crooked rows
scratched out
by three women,
sharing a space,
planting
lettuce, corn, peas.

> *Bells still call*
> *from the tower*
> *of Nuestra Doña de Guadalupe*
> *at Taos,*
> *calling los tres mujeres*
> *to look up from their jardín*
> *towards the sky and hum*
> *a prayer.*

Stringing Tobacco

Women in sunbonnets, stringing tobacco
In the hot North Carolina sun.
Nimble fingers pluck tobacco leaves
From an old wooden wagon bed,
Wrap twine around the stems,
Placing the leaves first on one side,
Then the other,
Of a smooth wooden pole,
Preparing the crop for the men to hang,
In the terrible heat of the drying shed.

Stringing done, chores at home wait.
There's water to be drawn
From the back porch well.
Before toting it inside, Grandma Boston
Reaches for a dented tin dipper,
Hanging on a nail,
Scoops a cool drink,
Tossing the remaining drops
Out into the yard,
To form tiny puddles of mud
Which quickly dry in the sun.

The women, slipping out of dusty shoes,
Enter the farmhouse
Built years ago, weathered by use.
Their hot bare feet refreshed
By soft pine planks —
A floor hollowed and smoothed
By generations of hot bare feet.

The older women share a dip of snuff,
Rest a spell in armless rockers
Before starting supper
On the black wood-stove.
Young granddaughters giggle, scuffle,
Tease for a dip —
Which their elders sternly ignore.

Before they can be directed
To bring stove kindling
Or fetch eggs from the hen house
The girls slip away to the tire swing,
Hanging idly, suspended from a slender pine.
Happily they play out of sight
Of their elders
In the waning twilight of summer.

Women's Memories Are Long

Three thousand years ago,
when I lived in Mesopotamia,
I wore my hair in one thick braid,
never cut it my life long —
though my life was not so long
as all that —
Eight children in ten years
left my body torn,
with a slow unstoppable bleeding,
seeping my cheeks from pink

to ashen gray,
while my children swirled around me,
sucking the last bit of nourishment,
as my life ebbed.

From a no-place I watched them
clean and wrap my body for burial.
Saw my long dark hair braided
for the last time,
saw my man and my children
shovel the earth
over my bloodless body,
saw the villagers help with food
and prayers, saw my man's black eyes
begin to search for his next woman.

Death Rushed By

Dressed in hospital whites,
gauze masks covering mouths
and noses, a man pulls,

a woman pushes a hospital
gurney. They rush through
the corridor, eyes carefully

averted from visitors, staff.
Atop the gurney, lies a sallow-
faced woman with white hair,

already diminished in size,
flat as a card in a Tarot deck.
At her feet are crumpled a bra,

panties, white cotton nightgown,
pink sweater. A pot of dead
yellow chrysanthemums carelessly

tossed across the body.

I Walked With You

I walked with you ten thousand
years ago in the Paleolithic.
Followed you along a deer trail,
cooked your meat over hot coals.
　I wonder why
　　you don't recognize me.

I walked with you in Persia
where you tended the flame
of Zoroaster. I wove
your robe in sunset colors.
　I wonder why
　　you don't recognize me.

I walked with you to a mountain
top in Zhongguo. We sipped hot
wine; wrote odes to the moon
in black ink.
　I wonder why
　　you don't recognize me.

I walked with you alongside
a covered wagon on the prairie,
birthed your child in a sod
hut and died.
　I wonder why
　　you don't recognize me.

I lie with you in a penthouse
In San Francisco, watch you toss,
turn, and settle into sleep,
　I wonder if in your dreams,
　　you recognize me.

Triangle

Love
always
involves
three — you,
me, & the woman
you think I am: The
one who loves getting
up an hour earlier to fix
you a hot breakfast; the one
who's eager for sex after a 12
hour work day; the one who listens
patiently while you complain once again
about the boss; the one who doesn't mind if
you ogle the shapely landlady; the one who cheer-
fully washes your dirty underwear. You know that
woman — but, lover, she's a complete stranger to me.

In The Clutches Of Roses

Victoria's secret is a wild
English garden enclosed
by old stone walls covered
with ivy, observed by robins
and nuthatches. Foxes
have a den in one hilly corner,
pass under the walls at night
to hunt furry rabbits, woodchucks.

Victoria grows roses and scandal
in her garden, meets a young
army officer with chest medals
in the gazebo at midnight,
he admires her rose-colored nipples
in white candle glow,
explains that his wife's nipples
have turned brown with childbearing,
no longer titillate.

The wild pink roses in the garden
turn brown with anger, sharpen
their thorns, creepingly surround
the gazebo. At dawn Victoria
covers her breasts with white
muslin, leaves her lover asleep,
his naked skin damp from passion.

After Victoria departs, the roses
grow and grow, cover the gazebo,
leave one small opening.
As the soldier attempts to crawl
through, carrying his battle dress,
thorns grow longer and sharper,
pierce his damp skin, hold him fast
until he withers, dies, turns to dust,
fertilizes the wild roses.

Haiku

a spiky-haired punk
dressed in black, carrying
a red poinsettia

 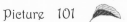

The Meaning Of Roses

The rose drooped, died, dropped
its red petals on varnished
oak table. The slender man,

a messenger from the past,
dissolved like sugar in a glass
of hot tea; man and rose leaving

no message, no twist from past
to present, no memory or scent
of roses, of man.

Tender petals, tender skin,
one pricking, one rasping,
the pain of softness.

No memory of rainy city streets
or wall-papered bedrooms.
Russian samovars and English

tea cozies float in the room
on rose-scented air currents,
bowls are filled with apricot

kernels, heated on candle flames.
A village of European peasants
step out from a Brueghel painting

point and accuse of patterns
deeper than love; messages
spiral, elusive as dreams

of red roses, their meaning
drifting upward in wisps
of smoke…

Loss Of A Mongoose

I have lost the names
of most of my grammar school
teachers
was there one named Mongoose?
no, maybe not
my fourth grade class picture
shows familiar faces but names
have vanished
names are the first to go
in the yellow honeycomb
of brain cells
will my own name
have been lost to me
when the last bell rings?

VII. Money

Money — A Ghazal

A red leather shoe can be used to adorn a slim foot.
It can also be sold for food or money.

Urashima, the fisher boy, sinks into the depths at the call of a
girl with no name.
When he left her to return to the world, the casket she gave
him contained suffering, old age, and death — but no money.

Locke argued that men/women must have consented to
inequalities of fortune and to possession without need.
After all, they invented money.

A beautiful translucent child is a newborn radiance.
There are those who trade them for money.

Constance, what do you know of gold coins, silver bullion?
You remain totally ignorant of the whimsy of money.

A banknote may describe to one person a drink in a pub,
to another a fairground ride, to a third a diamond ring.
An incarnate desire, they say, is money.

What is there that has the power to convey wishes?
The God of Our Times is Money.

How The Gaze Falls

The newest child in the family, the first of his generation,
is surrounded by aunts, uncles, parents, grandparents.
In the large room twenty-four eyes center on the boy

who reflects the loving gazes that hold him in the circle.
He plays with toys, pulls himself up to the coffee table.
A gentle group sigh greets his baby efforts.

We in the circle watch this shining child, our gazes brush
his chubby cheeks, his dimpled hands and knees. We consume
him like vanilla ice cream slathered with hot fudge.

All he does is our delight. Later, when in the midst
of my work, I have to recommend *or not* a guardian for a child,
I sit and talk to the child and the family who say they want him.

I watch the eyes of the adults. Do their eyes stray only briefly
from the child and then dart back to hold him safe in their sight
or do they ignore, look away, roll their eyes heavenward?

How loudly the gaze of love, of adoration sings in the eyes!
Where children are unloved, they fear the gaze that falls
on them, scurry like field mice, search for hiding holes,

to avoid the malevolent gaze that foretells their torture
or their death. They are not children of the right hearth,
the proper tribe, they fall victim to the gaze that obliterates.

All children deserve   deserve   the gaze of love
...all children...   ...everywhere...
Let adoration of the children   sing in the eye

Fear Of Opening

A brick was laid near the door
    ready for throwing.
The bearded man stood shadowy
    behind the screen door.
Gray clouds crowded in from the ocean.
The house hunkered in a neighborhood
    of old houses, old friends.
"Come no further," he yelled
    to all callers.

The sidewalk was still damp
    from the last rain.
The bearded man suffered
    no hallucinations.
Fear was the name of his prison.
A cool breeze herded wet leaves
    along the street.
The screen remained firmly shut,
    a brick lay ready to hand.

Erik

My burly son
with the sensitivity
of an artist
works at the all-night
Shell Station on Broadway.

He carries a gun
in his waistband.

A few blocks away
I lie in my bed
and hear the sounds
of the city night:
Gun shots, back-fires,
arguments, sirens.
The sounds float in
through my open window
and smother me with fear.

My son carries a gun
in his waistband.

He works alone
in the night's blackness
protected only by his
innocent courage, his trust
in his emerging manhood
and the gun
in his waistband.

I won't sleep
until the creak of the elevator
tells me he's home
safe for another night.

Song Of The Iguana

I'm sitting on a curb waiting
for an uptown bus when a tangerine
iguana, smelling of mint,
crawls up from the gutter
and over my leg. It sings me
a story of disappearing
children, shallow graves
riddled with bones,
of long ashen journeys,
searching for justice and safety.
I cradle the tangerine iguana,
smelling faintly of mint leaves,
rock it in my arms,
hum the song into my heart,
while we wait together
for the uptown bus.

Knife In The Throat

My neighbor, Lucilla, killed an attacking
dog by forcing a knife into its throat
one dark night, walking home from work

with friends. Lucilla and I would stand
on the sidewalk on a summer day, laughing,
talking, sharing a sense of humor.

We laughed at our own pain; were serious
about the pain of others. Lucilla told me
of packing her own vagina with raw cotton,

when, as a young girl, she began to hemorrhage,
while working in the cotton fields. There was never
a doctor. We stood, watching our children

play together, my son, her grandson. Once Lucilla
asked me to baby-sit while she turned a trick
for an old white man, a steady client years ago,

when she'd tricked for extra money: She laughed,
said she felt sorry for the old guy. Lucilla died
in Highland hospital of cancer of the throat.

I visited her before she died. She could scarcely
recognize me; could no longer talk or laugh.

Fuzzy Peaches

blush red on one curve
  golden green on the other

just peachy   nothing more fun
than a hot canning-peaches kitchen on a summer
  afternoon   90 in the shade

peaches on the table, the floor, in boiling
water   losing their skins
smell of peaches thick in humid air   peeling

hot skin from plump peaches   like skinning a live
thing   sticky on your fingers   juice falling
on paring knife   on apron   on floor

strands of hair brushed from face with sticky fingers
glued onto sweating brow   a canning peaches
sort of day   90 in the shade

Mother   earnest and pleased   filling hot jars
with hot peaches

other daughters are skipping to the beach
  riding bikes   hurrying to the movies
I am peeling endless lugs of peaches

        90 in the shade!

Mother   the thrifty housewife and   me
  in summer-HOT kitchen
boiling glass jars   peeling   slicing

when air-conditioned stores are filled
  with cans and cans and cans   of peaches

Smothering

I didn't know the cotton
got in your lungs,
smothered you.
I didn't know
Aunt Alice and Uncle Joe
were dying
of lung disease, yet,

I hurried by the mill;
I knew it could kill.

On the way to school
I walked by the brick
cotton mill and saw
cotton smothering
the windows,
like a billowy monster
trying to break out
into sunshine. Scared,

I hurried by the mill;
I knew it could kill.

I heard my aunts and uncles
speak with weariness
of the relentless work
in the summer heat
and the thick
cotton air that pressed
with its monster weight. Fearfully,

I hurried by the mill;
I knew it could kill.

VIII. Ambition

Ambition — A Ghazal

I yearn to live in New Mexico.
To lead a small life under large skies is my fond ambition.

Nine thousand year old bones have been found in the Northwest.
Who were the man's people, by what name was he known
and what were his ambitions?

China is threatening Tai-Wan again.
Is it only political rhetoric or is a nuclear outburst their
true ambition?

Two toddlers squabble over a red balloon that they haven't
learned to share.
To grasp a red balloon that dances in the air is their
fierce ambition.

Constance, only nine thousand year old bones are at peace.
Is the pull of deepest silence your final ambition?

A Frida Kahlo self-portrait shows her thick eyebrows
growing together.
A cave in her forehead holds a skull and bone, the height
of ambition.

Rip the sheets of poems from your notebook, toss them in the air.
A true poet is without ambition.

Tell A Lie About Yourself

I'm the girl-child of gypsies
who left me behind a torn
abandoned tent on the carnival
grounds when the carnival departed.

Inside the tent was a crystal
ball, shattered, lying strewn
on the floor of the ripped
abandoned tent. A dagger
with a small ruby in the handle
was also left behind.

The authorities, thoughtfully,
packed the dagger and the largest
piece of the crystal ball
into a brown paper sack,
delivered me and the sack
to Thelma and Joe Hester
of 1327 N. Main St., Newton, NC.

They delivered me at midnight.
My new parents embraced me,
fed me, bathed me, put me
to sleep between them under
quilts made by Joe's mother.
My new mother sang me to sleep.
The lullaby was, "Gone With
the Raggle, Taggle Gypsies, Oh."

Every summer, when I was old enough,
I wandered around the carnival,
when it came to town, looking
for gypsies, for fortune tellers.
Told no one I was searching.

Each summer when the carnival
departed, I'd walk through the empty
lot, watching for carnival treasures,
abandoned gypsy babies, my fingers
curling around a piece of crystal ball
that was always in my pocket. Mom
and Dad wouldn't let me carry
the ruby-hilted dagger.

First Music Lesson

I thought up lies all the way home,
watched my brown and white saddle shoes
not stepping on sidewalk cracks,
smelled fall rain gathering over
in Alexander County, felt it beginning
to move in my direction.

I crushed dried leaves beneath my feet,
didn't step on cracks, practiced lies,
trying to find the right one:

> There was no one home, Mother,
> I knocked on the door. No one
> answered.

> Mrs. Whitechapels' piano was
> being tuned, Mother, and she
> told me to come another day.

> Mrs. Whitechapel's daughter
> was hit by a car down at the
> Courthouse Square and an
> ambulance came and took her
> to the hospital and Mrs. White-
> chapel wasn't home because
> of the family emergency.

When I got home, Mother looked at me
in surprise and asked if piano lessons
were over so soon.

"I was scared to go in, Mother. I
just stood on the sidewalk. My feet
wouldn't take me in. I'm sorry,
Mother."

She hugged me tight and said
next time she'd go with me,

When I Longed For Horses

when I feared tidal waves, cowered in bed at 2 a.m.
   listened to storm-pushed breakers pounding cliff-sides

when my mother cooked big southern breakfasts
   of ham, eggs, grits, and red-eye gravy

when I longed for horses; read Black Beauty, King
   of the Wind, My Friend Flicka, and Thunderhead

when my breasts grew on my chest, round, soft, beautiful
   silken to the touch

when I rode bicycles, climbed trees,
   played with paper dolls

when my brother was born and I held him, sang to him,
   caroled *Silent Night* and he cried until I was silent

when I wrote stories of blonde-haired maidens and strong
   gentle knights

when I was thirteen and longed for horses.

July Parade

there is salt in the crook
of my elbow, my lover complains
as he thrusts me away

my cranberry nipples soften
I vibrate with anger
radiate a dull rose glow

I dash from his presence
lest he crush me like a blue python
hastily, I cover my alabaster breasts

and rump with yellow silk
hurry from his house
like a butterfly, I sail

down the city street, entering
the chaos of a July parade
I cherish the salt in the crook

of my elbow, am bored with thrusting
lovers, taunting men
the late afternoon light is mellow

on my skin, the music from school
bands elevates my mood
I flutter as the melody rises

lift my wings of yellow silk
I'm going somewhere. . .
yes, somewhere. . .

A Sky Falling Dream

For Anne and Catherine

I dreamed my daughter, Catherine,
was taller than the Kaiser Building.
She was looking down at me, shouting
from that long way off, "Mommy, Mommy,
put on your black boots and come
with me. Right now! The sky is falling
but I won't let it hit you."

My daughter picked me up in her right
hand, sat me on her shoulder. Her hair
hung loosely in blonde tangles,
I grabbed onto some curls, held tight.
She was so big.
Behind her head the sky was deep red
and falling.

"I'll take care of you, Mommy,
don't be afraid," Catherine said. Below
us, at her feet, was a line of yellow
school buses. Each one had the name
of a town painted on its side
in purple letters. They were towns
I'd never heard of: Showgo, Meemop,
Boggsie and Youyou.

Catherine walked out of town
with me on her shoulder, holding on
to her curls. The falling red sky
never hit us. Not once.

I Was Always Immense...

...danced, jitterbugged with universal
mind, grabbed a sax and wailed
with the bottomless sea, rode

the low notes of a tuba into earth's
deepest, most molten center, oh,
I grappled with Krishna, I soared

among the planets of Pluto and Uranus,
Neptune was the strangest,
my, the things that go on —

an entirely different atomic
level. I bowed a violin into ultimate
darkness, the hotter

I bowed the more immense I became.
I think there's no darned end to it
I explored violet for days and weeks,

found it covers the milky way.
Amber and turquoise
are worlds of their own,

whole worlds live in them.
I'm still expanding,
headed toward the remote eye

of a whirling tempest,
tasting bliss.

Accidental Buddha

It's the shape that attracts me

a tea bowl, hand-thrown by potters
who smash
              two hundred bowls

before their clear vision emerges

in the bowl's center a puddle of glaze
forms an accidental

Buddha

How can enlightenment not follow?

I've never found time to sit
on a planked floor
in a wooden pavilion set among pines
    and bamboo

never inhaled the steam of perfectly infused,
fragrant tea in a tea bowl
   with irregularities

never heard the whisk as it brushes
the tea, never sipped green tea down
   to a few bitter leaves

or found Buddha at the bottom
   of rust and sage bowl

Did I lack time or did I fear
I would find the tea bitter,
   flowers in the tokonomo
      artificial, tea bowl cracked —

only a glaze puddle at the center?

Song Of Bones

Let your mind walk
over the mesa toward Lama
where disciples sit zazen.

Let your mind walk
to the Rio Grande gorge
where two wild rivers
meet at La Junta.

Let your mind walk
in the midst
of bleached skulls
of tyrannosaurus, while
a pterodactyl's descendent
swoops aloft
in a canyon's updraft.

Let your mind walk
among crumbling walls
of cliff dwellers,
listen to the sweet
ghostly songs
of your ancestors.
Let your mind walk.

How Shall I Walk In The World?

I shall walk quietly
I shall walk without doing harm
I shall walk with music
I shall walk with my back straight
I shall walk, laughing
I shall walk, calling to a friend to walk with me
I shall walk with a book in my hand
I shall walk to a cafe and write a poem
I shall walk like a child
I shall walk, holding a child's hand
I shall walk in my old age with the vigor of my youth
I shall walk in the tracks of bear, deer, or rabbit
I shall walk in midnight and weep
I shall walk in grief
I shall walk in summer sunshine, swim in the sea
I shall walk up a mountain and take my mother with me
I shall walk with my father's arm around me
I shall walk, loving my sisters and my brother
I shall walk to the side of my sons and granddaughters
   whenever they need me
I shall walk in pure turquoise light
I shall walk in a painting of a blue barn,
   sleep in crimson hay
I shall walk into someone else's story and live it
I shall walk with memories
I shall walk into the future
I shall walk across the universe, using stars
   for stepping stones